The Unfortunate Fate of Bryan Christopher Kohberger

A Tale of Misfortune

Marcia J. Moreau

Marcia J. Moreau

Copyright©2022 Marcia J. Moreau
All right reserve

TABLE OF CONTENTS

TABLE OF CONTENTS

INTRODUCTION

BRYAN CHRISTOPHER KOHBERGER'S BIO
POLICE BREAK INTO A SUSPECT'S HOUSE.
KOHBERGER'S DEPRESSING EXAM STUDY
HE ATTENDED WASHINGTON STATE UNIVERSITY COLLEGE
HE AIDED IN STUDENT INSTRUCTION
PERSONAL INFORMATION
CRIMINAL BEHAVIOR
BRYAN KOHBERGER'S HISTORY OF OFFENSES
NO LOGICAL CONNECTION TO CASUALTIES
LESS WELL-KNOWN REALITY THE CROOK
VICTIMS
IS KAYLEE GONCALVES'S EX-BOYFRIEND A SUSPECT?
HAS THE SUSPECT'S FAMILY SPOKEN TO HIM OR HER ABOUT BEING CAPTURED?
HOW WERE EACH OTHER KNOWN TO THE COLLEGE OF IDAHO CASUALTIES?
HOW DID THE VICTIMS OF THE COLLEGE OF IDAHO MURDERS PASS AWAY?

Marcia J. Moreau

INTRODUCTION

Six weeks after four College of Idaho students were brutally murdered, authorities have apprehended Bryan Christopher Kohberger, 28.

A PhD in criminal science who has been charged with the murders of four College of Idaho interns is currently facing a potential capital homicide trial.

According to papers obtained by The Autonomous, Bryan Christopher Kohberger, 28, was apprehended on December 30 in north-eastern Pennsylvania by agents of the FBI and Pennsylvania State Police close to the Pocono Mountains.

The Moscow Police Division and the Latah District Examiner's Office have filed a first-degree murder complaint against the Washington State College student, and he is being kept in custody pending removal.

The 21-year-olds Madison Mogen and Kaylee Goncalves, as well as 20-year-olds Xana Kernodle and Ethan Chapin, were apprehended on November 13 in a Moscow, Idaho, understudy home. This was their first significant forward movement in a long time.

On Friday, December 30, Moscow police appeared to rule out another suspect in a public interview.

James Fry, the head of the Moscow police, said, "We have a guy in guardianship who conducted these dreadful wrongdoings and I honestly do accept our local region is protected, but we actually need be careful.

The 25,000-person city had been living in fear due to the heinous concept of the crimes and the obvious lack of movement from the authorities.

Bryan Christopher Kohberger's bio

According to administrative work related to the suspect's capture that Pennsylvania State Police reported in Monroe Area Court, the suspect's identity is Bryan Christopher Kohberger.

According to the capture documents, Mr. Kohberger was apprehended by a specialized team at 3am on Friday in the Pocono Mountains of Pennsylvania's Monroe Province.

Bryan Christopher Kohberger, 28, was apprehended in connection with the murders of four College Idaho students.

Due to the consequences, he must deal with being sent to Idaho.

NBC News said that police were following a white Hyundai Elantra from the location where Mr. Kohberger was apprehended.

After being taken into custody, the suspect "asked if anyone else had been taken into custody," CNN Nation writer Brian Entin wrote on Twitter.

He was said to have a "calm, clear look."

According to the Washington State College website, Mr. Kohberger is a PhD understudy at the Pullman, Washington, law enforcement and criminal science office.

The understudies lived in Moscow, Idaho, about nine miles (15 km) west of Pullman.

According to court documents, Bryan Kohberger, a criminal science student at Washington State College, has been apprehended in connection with the murders of four students from the College of Idaho.

In May 2022, Mr. Kohberger graduated from DeSales College in Pennsylvania with a degree in law enforcement.

Online academic records show that Mr. Kohberger graduated from Northampton Junior College in Albrightsville with a partner management degree in 2018 and from DeSales College with a masters degree in law enforcement this year.

His mother was listed as a paraprofessional at Lovely Valley School Region, where he was employed part-time as a safety officer until August 2021.

According to Amanda's Facebook page, she also left Wonderful Valley Secondary School.

While his other sister, Melissa, works as a consultant in New Jersey, she currently fills in as a behavior expert and specialist in Bethlehem.

Police break into a suspect's house.

Following Mr. Kohberger's arrest in Pennsylvania, authorities carried out a court order on the suspect's apartment in Pullman, Washington, according to Fox News.

At 7.30am, specialists in a few unmarked vehicles arrived at the scene, according to nearby residents who spoke to Fox News.

When authorities arrived at the property, the scene was taped off with police tape. Bill Thompson, an examiner from Latah Region in Idaho, was one of the inspectors that combed over the property.

Jason LaBar, Mr. Kohberger's public defender, has declared that he will delay Mr. Kohberger's removal rights when he appears at the Monroe Region Town Hall in Stroudsburg, Pennsylvania, on Tuesday night.

Kohberger's depressing exam study

Approximately six months before, Mr. Kohberger oversaw a review in which criminals were questioned about how they selected their goals and how they felt while committing the crimes.

In a since-deleted Reddit post from May, he wrote: "Hi, I'm Bryan and I'm welcome you to take part in an examination project that aims to appreciate how feelings and mental features effect decision-production while carrying out a crime." "This research specifically attempts to ascertain the circumstances surrounding your most recent criminal offense, with emphasis on your attitudes and feelings throughout your experience."

Unknown reviewers asked questions such as "Did you prepare for the wrongdoing before leaving your home?" "For what reason did you choose that casualty or focus over others?" and "What was the first move you made to attain your objective?"

What were you thinking and feeling after committing the offense, he further questioned?

While Mr. Kohberger was focusing on criminal science, where such inquiries could seem to be an important component of any program, many people might view them differently after his capture in relation to the murders of Mogen, Goncalves, Kernodle, and Chapin.

studying and living in college

He attended Washington State University College

Bryan Christopher Kohberger, now 28 years old and born in November 1994, was taken into custody on Friday at a residence in Chestnut Hill Municipality in the Monroe

District of Pennsylvania. He is from Albrightsville, a nearby community in a neighboring district, according to a court record. Kohberger is a Ph.D. candidate at Washington State College with a focus on criminal justice and law enforcement, the university said on Friday. According to WSU, Kohberger recently completed his most memorable semester while a Ph.D. understudy in the law enforcement section before. The understudies were fatally injured on November 13 at a home on Ruler Street in Moscow, Idaho, which is about 9 miles west of the school's Pullman, Washington, location. At a news conference on Friday, police revealed that Kohberger resided in Pullman. Kohberger, Bryan C. posted by WSU Bryan Kohberger is an alumnus who is currently a student at Washington State College in Pullman's law enforcement and criminal science department.

He aided in student instruction

Kohberger is listed as an associate instructor for three undergraduate law enforcement courses taught by teacher John Snyder, the division's law enforcement club consultant and global chief, in the autumn course index for Washington Express College. The online course list shows that the three courses were finished on December 9. Snyder, who was reached Friday on his cellphone, declined to comment and sent an Idaho Legislator journalist to the college. The school thanked the police for helping those affected by the deaths express their sentiments in a statement, but made no more comments about Kohberger other than to confirm his enlistment. If Kohberger was employed by the university and resided in university housing, WSU did not specify. Requests for information sent via message to Kohberger's three individual Ph.D. students listed as assistant teachers for the college classes, the law enforcement division's seat, its alumni program director, and the alumni understudy affiliation counsel were not promptly responded to.

He was a Pennsylvania native. A community called Albrightsville can be found in eastern Pennsylvania's Pocono Mountains. In Monroe Province, just to the east of the New Jersey state line and about 75 miles west of New York City, Kohberger was held captive. According to records kept by the educational committee, a man by the name of Bryan Kohberger began working part-time as a "relaxed security official" for the Wonderful Valley School Region in the Monroe District in November 2018. The Pocono Record reported in 2018 that Kohberger procured an AED for a secondary school student who was experiencing a medical emergency. In August 2021, Kohberger was replaced by a permanent security officer. He recently left a school in Pennsylvania. In 2018, Kohberger graduated with a partner of expressions degree in brain science from Northampton Junior College in Pennsylvania, according to Mia Rossi-Marino, a representative of the institution. The AP reported that after enrolling at DeSales College in Allentown, Pennsylvania, he graduated with a four-year certification in 2020.

Albrightsville is about 40 miles south of Allentown. In May 2022, Kohberger obtained a master's degree in expressions in law enforcement while still employed at DeSales, according to Carolyn Steigleman, partner VP of communications. In an email to the legislator, Steigleman stated, "On Friday, December 30, DeSales College learned of Bryan Kohberger's capture regarding the homicide of four College of Idaho understudies. "As a Salesian, Catholic people group, we are devastated by this absurd disaster. During this difficult moment, our prayers and thoughts are with the families of the victims." According to the college's website, DeSales was founded by followers of St. Francis de Deals, a Catholic saint who "felt that affection for God drives normally to cherish for all others." He had never committed a crime. Kohberger had only one infraction for failing to buckle up in the Latah District, which includes Moscow, in August 2022, according to a search of court records in Washington, Idaho, and Pennsylvania. Kohberger currently expects to be fired from the Monroe Area Remedial Office. Latah Region Examiner Bill Thompson informed reporters at a news conference on Friday that he must deal with four first-degree murder charges as well as a legitimate offense robbery accusation. According to a court file, Kohberger was scheduled to appear in Monroe Region court on Tuesday at 1:30 PM Mountain time for a removal hearing. If Kohberger rejects willful removal, Idaho Governor Brad Little would have to request it from Pennsylvania, which would delay Kohberger's transfer to Idaho.

Personal Information

Is Bryan Kohberger Married?

Who is Bryan Kohberger's spouse?

Bryan Kohberger was last known to be married in 2022.

Bryan Kohberger is dating.

The status of Bryan Kohberger's relationships and sweetheart are frequently discussed online. Kohberger, however, provides no information about his friend. He might be single (starting around 2022). Bryan enjoys spending time with his friends. Additionally, there are a few images of Bryan with his friends online. When we have information about his better half, we will update this page.

Guardians of Bryan Kohberger

Maryann Kohberger and Michael Kohberger Jr. were responsible for bringing Kohberger into the world.

Bryan Koyhberger's guardians are similar to those of his two older sisters, Amanda and Melissa.

young Bryan Kohberger

Kohberger is not yet known to have children.

Level of Bryan Kohberger

Do you require Bryan Kohberger Level? Read this article to learn more details about Bryan Kohberger Level after that. Bryan Kohberger was born on November 21, 1994, and is a student, media personality, and business visionary. Recently, we've noticed fans searching for Bryan Kohberger level.

The subtleties of Bryan Kohberger's level and background are those that clients search for the most. People who have been wondering what Bryan Kohberger's level is can refer to the information below.

The fans are currently aware of Bryan Kohberger's height. Refer to the table below to learn about Bryan Kohberger's account.

Name Kohberger, Bryan

I'm calling the understudy, the media personality, and the businessperson

Date of Birth: 21 November 1994

Mature (starting around 2023) (starting around 2023) I'm 28 years old.

Level 172 cm

Marcia J. Moreau

65 kg

Total assets USD 100K-150K

Bryan Kohberger the Understudy, Media Face, and Business visionary was brought into the world on 21 November 1994, coming to Bryan Kohberger age according to surprise sports Bryan Kohberger is 28 years of age. Bryan Kohberger has earned recognition and furthermore acquired a great deal of supporters. Presently we should fast get into the article to discover how tall is Bryan Kohberger and much more nuances.

How tall is Bryan Kohberger?

Individuals who are desperate to know Bryan Kohberger Level can actually glance at this portion. As noted above, Bryan Kohberger's level in Centimeters is 172 cm. Regarding Bryan Kohberger's careers, he has been a successful understudy, media personality, and businessman. Bryan Kohberger, who was born on November 21, 1994, is now 28 years old and weighs 65 kg.

Weight of Bryan Kohberger

Understudy, media personality, and businessman Bryan Kohberger stands tall. Bryan Kohberger weighs 65 kg, and as of roughly 2023, he will be 28 years old. Along with these details, we have also provided Bryan Kohberger Total Assets; see the following section to find out how much Bryan Kohberger Total Assets are.

Total assets of Bryan Kohberger

What is the total value of Bryan Kohberger's assets? A WSU educational collaborator is Bryan Christopher Kohberger. He also puts an emphasis on his academics. In any event, there is no information available on his specific occupation. The estimated value of Kohberger's entire assets is between $100,000 and $150,000. (approx.).

Former friends of the suspect react to his capture

Former friends and coworkers of Mr. Kohberger have approached with insights about his character and his upsetting past, which they claim is distinguished by heroin addiction and weight struggles, in the wake of the leading edge capture almost seven weeks after the brutal stabbings.

Sara Healey, a former classmate of Mr. Kohberger's from secondary school, said on Friday on Fox News Advanced, "It was horrific." "He seemed to have something terribly off about him, though we couldn't put our finger on what. I remember one time he stopped me as I was walking down the hall and asked, "Would you like to hang out?""

She added: "However Bryan was harassed a ton, and I never had an opportunity to express something to guard him, since he would constantly take off."

Notwithstanding his battles, Mr. Kohberger was extremely savvy and consistently had passing marks, Ms. Healey said. She added that Mr. Kohberger was frequently dismissed and harassed by females, persuading her to think it was that inward disappointment which eventually prompted his supposed association in the Moscow assault.

Another secondary school friend of Mr. Kohberger claimed that the accused murderer became a "domineering jerk" in his senior year as a way to deal with his personal weaknesses.

"Usually, he had to fight someone because he was bothering everyone. We decided to remove him from our group of friends because he was very different from us "The Day to Day Monster was informed by Scratch Mcloughlin.

Mr. Kohberger also experienced a remarkable weight loss that year, according to Mr. Mcloughlin.

Another student from Mr. Mcloughlin's secondary school cohort, Thomas Arntz, reiterated his description of Mr. Kohberger as a harasser.

Mr. Arntz told the distribution, "He did that to me all the time." "He would seek out my information. He would effectively imply that I'm too ignorant and absent-minded and slow on the uptake of information to be his buddy."

A coworker of Mr. Kohberger's at Northampton Junior College in Pennsylvania, who asked to remain anonymous, told Fox News Computerized that she last spoke with him about a year or so ago to discuss their expectations for their academic futures.

She assured Mr. Kohberger that she would spend hours counseling him about his heroin addiction and that he would be pursuing his PhD.

"He's so clever it's crazy. A talented young person who shone out in all circles and major level classes, "She informed the group. "I need to talk to him right away and find out what was going on. What went terribly wrong? What were you thinking at the time? What emotions did you have? What was going on? You know, why do you suppose that occurred?"

In May 2022, Mr. Kohberger graduated from DeSales College in Pennsylvania with a degree in law enforcement.

Mr. Kohberger's DeSales schoolmate told The Daily Beast about a time when he had a disagreement with the arrested suspect.

"He was quite evened out and somewhat imposing. He didn't express himself very well, "they claimed. He was careful in his speech.

According to a statement to the media, the school said: "DeSales College heard on Friday, December 30, of Bryan Kohberger's arrest in connection with the murder of four College of Idaho interns. Kohberger completed his alumni concentrates in June 2022 after receiving a four-year certification in 2020. We, a Salesian Catholic people organization, are appalled by this absurd disaster. The families of the casualties are in our thoughts and prayers during this trying time."

Kohberger allegedly made "unpleasant" comments to the female employees of the brewery.

Mr. Kohberger, who resided not far from the Pullman grounds, had returned to Pennsylvania to spend important occasions with his loved ones.

Jordan Serulnec, 34, the owner of Seven Alarms Blending Company in Bethlehem, Dad, told NBC News in a report published this week's end that Mr. Kohberger was notorious for making inappropriate comments to female clients and employees.

When customers' IDs are filtered, the company provides a framework that enables employees to submit notes to their profiles. After reading what his employees had to say about Mr. Kohberger, Mr. Serulnec made the decision to confront the now-accused murderer.

"The staff posted: "Hello, be on the lookout for this person as he makes frightening comments. He'll have a few beers and then become overly familiar," "Serulnec told NBC this.

Added him: "I became reliant on him and greeted Bryan by saying, "Hello, welcome back." We appreciate you coming back. I just needed to have a quick conversation with you to make sure that you understand this time and that there won't be any problems. He was very shocked, too. He expressed shock that I was stating that and said, "I have no idea." You have completely confused me."

In the fourfold homicide investigation in Moscow, Idaho, Bryan Kohberger, 28, is a suspect.

Mr. Serulnec continued by saying that Mr. Kohberger would become upset if the businesswomen turned down his sincere advances. On one specific occasion, when a member of the staff didn't react to his questions, he considered it a "defaming phrase."

Months before those incidents, Mr. Serulnec told NBC that Mr. Kohberger didn't return to his job after being disobeyed.

Criminal behavior

Suspect's family "shaken" by shooting at Uvalde School

MaryAnn Kohberger, Mr. Kohberger's mother, recently wrote a letter to the Pocono Record lamenting the atrocities in Uvalde and elsewhere.

"I struggled with what steps to take to stop the hysteria earlier today as I sat, reeling after yet another school shooting. What's the answer? measures to regulate weapons? Mediation for emotional well-being "She stated in a letter that was published on June 2.

Then, she continued, "I received a message from my young daughter who fills in as an emotional wellbeing consultant in New Jersey.

She shared a sonnet that she had written while experiencing the depths of despair.

It had a significant impact on me, therefore I wanted to share it:

Uvalde, Texas, May 24, 2022, music by Melissa Kohberger

deprived of their giggling

There is no sound at the moment.

as we bury our children in the ground

little feet and hands

the world that bombed them was buried six feet beneath the surface of the earth.

As I was reading the sonnet, Ms. Kohberger said, "Anything that the arrangement, I urge we think of the kids before the guns."

Sunday saw the deaths of Ethan Chapin, 20, Madison Mogen, 21, Xana Kernodle, 20, and Kaylee Goncalves, 21.

Bryan Kohberger, a security guard at Lovely Valley, received praise from a comparable publication for his efforts to assist a spouse going through a health crisis.

DeSales College and the Charming Valley school district have been contacted by the Autonomous for comments.

The Kohberger family did not swiftly respond to messages left with them.

A case that engulfed the nation and perplexed police

For a month and a half after the murders, investigators were unable to identify a suspect or locate a lethal weapon.

The first significant development occurred when authorities asked for the public's help in locating a white vehicle that had been sighted nearby the scene of the killings.

Despite receiving a large number of entries on its website, the Moscow Police Division claimed to have received more than 13,000 telephone tips related to the case.

He allegedly used heroin while a high student.

Some of Kohberger's coworkers from his children reported seeing him use heroin, and some claimed that Kohberger sold the drug to others before seeking help in 2013. After meeting Kohberger at a party, Lee Mack, who graduated from Charming Valley Secondary School in 2012, told Individuals that they became friends.

"I'm not aware of Bryan ever emitting any warning signals. He was always strange, but the typical high school student trying to fit in isn't strange, you know? "Kohberger briefly joined her group of companions, she observed, but they split up after Kohberger allegedly offered another friend heroin.

He offered my closest friend heroin, and we recently realized he was somewhat further along than we had anticipated, so we had to end our friendship, Mack said. Two years after graduating, Kohberger reconnected with her, she continued. 'Hello,' he said. I'm becoming pristine. I think it ought to benefit me and other people.

Kohberger holds a degree in brain research.

The New York Times reported that Kohberger earned a four-year certification in brain science at a local junior college close to his former neighborhood in eastern Pennsylvania.

Kohberger was very interested in brain science as a child, according to Jack Baylis, a friend of Kohberger's since the eighth grade.

He asks a lot of questions. Most likely the most inquisitive [person] you will ever meet. "Ensured," said Baylis. He was deeply interested in brain science, human cognition, and other topics. He has always been really into that kind of stuff.

"Let's say you're thinking, 'Goodness, why do people really behave in this manner? What causes men to "yakked yak?" "Or what causes women to "yakked yak?" He would get quite interested in topics like that, comparing how different people thought, and other such things, Baylis continued.

Baylis, who last saw Kohberger in 2021 when they fired airsoft weapons together, understood that it hasn't been easy to accept the thought that his beloved buddy could be held accountable for the deaths of four young adults.

"He has always been kind to me and continuously accommodating. Never seemed to cause issue, according to Baylis. "I want to think that he is innocent. I have faith that it was someone else. because you don't think your friend should have killed. It is horrible.

DeSales College awarded him a graduate degree in law enforcement.

In a statement, DeSales College confirmed that Kohberger was a graduate. A note on the college website stated, "Kohberger got a four year college education in 2020 and ended his alumnus concentrates in June 2022." Kohberger holds a graduate degree in criminal justice.

"This ridiculous misfortune has left us crushed. We can also see the potential impact this news may have on the economic health of our community. DeSales has expanded its direction services for students, employees, and staff, the statement continued.

We extend deep sympathy and pleas to the relatives of the individuals in question as a Catholic, Salesian people group.

When Kohberger was a student at DeSales, he published a since-deleted Reddit post inviting ex-offenders to participate in what he claimed was a college evaluation on how "feelings and mental attributes effect decision-production while executing a violation."

Brittany Slaven, one of his DeSales coworkers, told The New York Times that Kohberger seemed to be quite interested in serial killers and developing theories about what happened at crime scenes based on images shown in class, but that his behavior did not alarm her at the time. She explained, "At the time, he may have merely been an inquisitive understudy, so if his questioning were unusual we didn't respect it since it suited our teaching agenda.

Casey Arntz observed Kohberger's interest in law enforcement when he was still in high school, but she recognized that his habit delayed his plans to enter college so he could focus on the subject.

She claimed, "He most definitely was interested in police enforcement back then. Additionally, I'm learning from other people that former friends, coworkers, and even teachers who knew him indicated that he was always interested in it and that he loved bad-faith programs and movies, among other things.

Kohberger received a warning from a local pub months before the killings.

A while earlier, Kohberger received a warning regarding his associations with women who frequented and worked at a pub in Bethlehem, Dad. Owner of Seven Alarms Blending Organization Jordan Serulneck spoke to NBC News.

Serulneck understood that the bar staff checks the IDs of all patrons and that they can record any new observations that emerge in their internal framework. "Staff wrote, 'Hello, this person makes terrible comments; be on the lookout for him. He'll drink a few beers and then become overly accustomed,' Serulneck analyzed.

The owner of the distillery claimed that Kohberger frequently sat alone at the bar "noticing and monitoring" various patrons and that he inquired about the residences of female staff members and customers as well as who they were at the bar with. Serulneck claimed that if women were reluctant to converse, Kohberger "would go off the handle with them a tad" and that Kohberger referred to a female employee as a "b—" when she refused to answer his questions.

Regarding his previous relationship with Kohberger, Serulneck remarked, "I went dependant upon him and I said, "Hello Bryan, welcome back. We appreciate you coming back. I just needed to talk to you really quickly to make sure you'll be aware this time and we won't run into any problems. Kohberger reportedly expressed shock at Serulneck's remarks and informed the business owner, "I don't have a clue. I'm completely confused by you.

Kohberger, according to Serulneck, never returned to the pub following the conversation.

Kohberger claimed that the allegations against him left him "stunned."

Jason LaBar, a public safety officer for Monroe County, Texas, told CNN that Kohberger was "a little bit startled" by the accusations.

Kohberger would defer his right to a removal hearing in an effort to get closer to his absolution, according to LaBar, who spoke with Kohberger for the removal procedures but is not his attorney in the criminal case.

In view of the fact that he expects to be excused, he will forgo, LaBar explained. "That was what he said. Whether or whether that means he is blameless, it is indicated by the statement that he needs to be absolved. He avoided using the word "honest.""

Bryan Kohberger's history of offenses

Kohberger is being held in custody because he is the top suspect in the horrifying murders of four students at the College of Idaho in the United States of America.

The victims killed by Mr. Kohberger included Ethan Chapin, 20, of Conway, Washington, Kaylee Goncalves, 21, of Rathdrum, Idaho, Xana Kernodle, 20, of Avondale, Arizona, and Madison Mogen, 21, of Coeur d'Alene, Idaho.

They were all College of Idaho undergrads. The two seniors were Goncalves and Mogen, Kernodle was a weaker player, and Chapin was a first-year recruit.

The tragic incident is alleged to have taken place on November 13th, 2022, while the four understudies slept in an off-grounds, three-story leased property in Moscow, Idaho.

A number of College of Idaho students resided in an off-campus investment home in Moscow, Idaho, a sleepy town with a small university. The three-story house has two rooms on each floor. There hadn't been a murder committed in that mindset since roughly 2015, until the most recent incident.

On November 13, 2022, between the hours of 3:00 and 4:00 am, four College of Idaho undergraduates were fatally injured at a shared investment property close to the university, where three of them lived.

The three women killed at the house were Xana Kernodle, Kaylee Goncalves, and Madison Mogen. Kernodle's boyfriend, Ethan Chapin, was present on the attack night.

They slept through the assaults in safety at the same residence as the two other female roommates. Chapin and

Kernodle, two of the four victims, attended a party at the nearby Sigma Chi crew on the evening of November 12 between the lengthy hours of 8 and 9. They got back home at 1:45 a.m.

The other two victims that night were close friends Mogen and Goncalves, who left a city tavern where they had gone to play games at 1:30 in the morning.

Mogen and Goncalves were seen conversing and beaming at 1:41 in the morning in a live Jerk stream from The Grub Truck, a food truck four traffic lights away at Fellowship Square (Fundamental and Fourth Roads). They accepted their food after ten minutes, and then they departed to take what the police initially believed to be an Uber ride home, a roughly one mile detour (1.6 km). Each of the four understudies returned by 1:56 in the morning. In the early hours of the day, between the hours of 2:26 and 2:52, Goncalves made seven ineffective phone calls to her ex, a single student.

Mogen repeatedly approached the beau from 2:44 to 2:52 in the initial portion of the day, with the same outcomes each time. After looking into these calls, the police came to the conclusion that he wasn't responsible for the wrongdoing.

The deaths took place in the two remaining flatmates' rooms on the ground level of the house; they had arrived home around one AM. They didn't arrive till another time at the start of the day, neither were they pursued or abducted.

The four casualties were shot to death on the second and third levels of the home, where they were sleeping. The victims were not restrained or strangled, and there was blood all over the nearby walls.

Nobody called 911 until 11:58 am, several hours after the early morning murders. Around that time, one of the additional residents' cellphones inside the unit was used to place a call for assistance for a "oblivious" person.

When the police arrived, the entrance to the house was unlocked, nothing seemed to have been taken, and there were no obvious signs of restricted access or property damage within the home. The two surviving flatmates as well as some of the victims' coworkers were present when the cops arrived.

The remaining flatmates invited friends around because they knew one of the casualties on the upper floor was lethargic and not stimulating.

Each of the four victims was pronounced dead around 12 o'clock. That evening, authorities discovered Goncalves' dog in the house; it was later delivered to what the police described as a "party in question." This dog was a gift from Goncalves to her ex.

Kohberger was detained by the Pennsylvania State Police and the FBI on December 30 in Chestnuthill Municipality, Monroe Province, Pennsylvania.

no logical connection to casualties

The suspects are seniors Madison Mogen, 21, of Coeur d'Alene, and Kaylee Goncalves, 21, of Rathdrum; junior Xana Kernodle, 20, of Post Falls; and first-year recruit Ethan Chapin, 20, of Mount Vernon, Washington. Police have not uncovered any prior connections between Kohberger and the suspects. Ethan's mother, Stacy Chapin, wrote to the legislator to say that her family is unaware of any connection between Ethan and the suspect. A former member of a sorority at the University of Illinois who formerly resided in the Ruler Street neighborhood and who agreed to remain anonymous stated Kohberger was unknown to some of the people in question's friends. "Never heard of him or seen him before. She stated Friday in a Facebook post to the Legislator, "Nobody I know knows him. Mogen and Kernodle belonged to Pi Beta Phi, whereas Goncalves belonged to the sorority Alpha Phi.

Less well-known reality THE CROOK

He lived in Pullman, Washington before being apprehended at his parents' residence, for example.

2. Despite never being apprehended, he was briefly mentioned for not using a safety belt.

3. He used to go on night runs with a friend named Schyler Jacobson, and the two of them would cover a good distance together.

4. He is a criminal science Ph.D. candidate.

5. He served as an adjunct professor for three classes at Washington College.

6. He has drab, earthy-colored hair and green eyes.

7. He practices the Christian faith.

8. He identifies as American.

9. He has multiple identities.

10. Scorpio is his zodiac sign.

Victims

Is the bartender a suspect in the murders at the College of Idaho?

Goncalves and Mogen were captured in an observation video that Fox News Computerized released on Saturday, December 17, talking about a man named "Adam" while strolling through midtown Moscow just hours before the killings.

Steve Goncalves, Goncalves' father, asserted that Adam is unquestionably not a suspect.

On the December 17 episode of Lawrence Jones Cross-country, he said, "We asked and did the conspicuously expected level of effort, and that's what we investigated, and it was evident that this individual was not a piece of the examination to the extent that a suspect."

Adam has since gained notoriety as a local bartender, according to TMZ.

Is Kaylee Goncalves's ex-boyfriend a suspect?

As Jack DuCoeur and Kaylee had dated for a long time and only ended their relationship three weeks before the murders, he was once thought to be a person of interest in the killings. However, his auntie discovered that despite his grief over Kaylee's absence, he was "crushed" by people's suspicions of him.

"He's not just lost his first love, and what we all suspected and presumably thought too, would be his future spouse —

you know, get married and have children and all of that," Jack's aunt Brooke Mill operator told Page Six on December 24. "In addition, 'a big part of America' figures he could 'be mindful' for the killings."

The mill operator revealed that although he was clearly miserable, they were still friends and that Kaylee "was anticipating moving forever" and that their breakup was "genial."

At first, Jack was thought to be a person of interest in the killings because Kaylee and Madison tried to call DuCoeur several times before they were killed along with their other flatmate Xana Kernoodle and Kernoodle's sweetheart, Ethan Chapin, but Jack didn't answer.

After looking into the conversations, experts in Moscow, Idaho "cleared" Jack and stated on November 23 that he was not generally thought to be a suspect.

Tragically, many online sleuths agree that Jack was involved in the murders and have expressed a few theories via virtual amusement as to why they believe he is the murderer. The idea was pounded home by Jack's aunt.

The mill operator remarked, "They're just the silliest stunts." We all agree that it is essentially impossible for Jack to ever harm somebody in this way, and we know this without a doubt.

Since Kaylee's passing, Jack has also received open support from Kaylee's mother, father, and sister.

Has the suspect's family spoken to him or her about being captured?

According to Individuals, Kohberger's legal representative Jason A. LaBar declared in a proclamation for the suspect's father Michael Kohberger, mother Marianne Kohberger, and sister Amanda on January 2, 2023, "Most importantly, we care profoundly for the four families who have lost their valuable kids."

They said, "We supplicate every day for them since there are no words that can adequately express the agony we feel. We will continue to let the legal relationship develop, and as a family, we will value and uphold our child and sister.

In the explanation, they highlighted that they had "totally assisted policing trying to look for reality and promote his idea of blamelessness as opposed to pass judgment on murky realities and make erroneous suspicions." "Our family and the families suffering hardship can go forward through the legal procedure," the statement reads.

How Were Each Other Known to the College of Idaho Casualties?

In the home where the victims were discovered, Mogen, Kernodle, and Goncalves shared a flat. Although Chapin didn't live there, at the time of the accident he was dating

Kernodle. The three women all belonged to sororities, whereas Chapin was a member of a crew.

How did the victims of the College of Idaho murders pass away?

Police tracked down the four victims on the second and third levels of the house after they were injured on separate occasions with a large fixed-edge blade. The casualties were reportedly sleeping at the time of the attack, according to the coroner, but several had defensive wounds and may have tried to fend off the assailant. In their opinion, there was no evidence of rape.

Marcia J. Moreau

www.ingramcontent.com/pod-product-compliance
Lightning Source LLC
Chambersburg PA
CBHW050323220526
45465CB00005B/2112